THE LITTLE GIANT BOOK OF

Knock-Knocks

Charles Keller

Illustrated by Sanford Hoffman

Sterling Publishing Co., Inc.
New York

Library of Congress Cataloging-in-Publication Data

Keller, Charles.
      Little giant book of knock-knocks / Charles Keller ; illustrated by Sanford Hoffman.
         p.   cm.
      Includes index.
      Summary: A collection of hundreds of knock-knock jokes, arranged alphabetically.
      ISBN 0-8069-8108-3
      1.Knock-knock jokes. 2. Wit and humor, Juvenile.
[1. Knock-knock jokes. 2. Jokes.] I. Hoffman, Sanford, ill. II. Title.
PN6231.K55K43 1997
818'.5402–dc21
                                     96–40058
                                     CIP
                                     AC

10 9 8 7 6 5 4 3 2 1

Published by Sterling Publishing Company, Inc.
387 Park Avenue South, New York, N.Y. 10016
© 1997 by Charles Keller
Distributed in Canada by Sterling Publishing
℅ Canadian Manda Group, One Atlantic Avenue, Suite 105
Toronto, Ontario, Canada M6K 3E7
Distributed in Great Britain and Europe by Cassell PLC
Wellington House, 125 Strand, London WC2R 0BB, England
Distributed in Australia by Capricorn Link (Australia) Pty Ltd.
P.O. Box 6651, Baulkham Hills, Business Centre, NSW 2153,
    Australia
Manufactured in the United States of America
Sterling ISBN 0-8069-8108-3

Contents

To Gabriel

ACKNOWLEDGMENTS
I would like to acknowledge the help of and give special thanks to Steve Blance, Rhoda Crispell, Robert Farhi, Brenda Gordon, Keith Planit, and Philip Recchia.

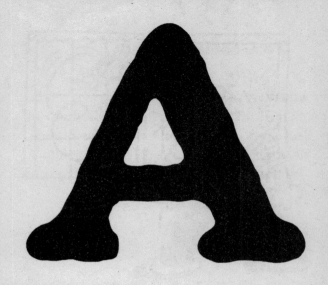

Knock-knock.
  Who's there?
A-1
  A-1 who?
A-1 to know.

♠ ♦ ➡ ♦ ⬇ ◆

Knock-knock.
  Who's there?
Abbe.
  Abbe who?
Abbe stung me on the nose.

Knock-knock.
   Who's there?
Abbot.
   Abbot who?
Abbot you don't know who I am.

Knock-knock.
   Who's there?
Abby.
   Abby who?
"Abby seeing you in all the old familiar places…"

Knock-knock.
   Who's there?
Abby and Manny.
   Abby and Manny who?
Abby birthday and Manny happy returns.

Knock-knock.
  Who's there?
Ach.
  Ach who?
Gesundheit.

Knock-
knock.
  Who's there?
Ahab.
  Ahab who?
Ahab a cold in my nose.

Knock-knock.
  Who's there?
Acid.
  Acid who?
Acid down, you're rocking the boat.

✦ ↗ ➜ ◪ ⬇ ◣

Knock-knock.
  Who's there?
Adam.
  Adam who?
Adam up and send me the bill.

✦ ↗ ➜ ◪ ⬇ ◣

Knock-knock.
  Who's there?
Adele.
  Adele who?
Adele is where the farmer lives.

✦ ↗ ➜ ◪ ⬇ ◣

Knock-knock.
  Who's there?
Adios.
  Adios who?
Adios me some money.

  ↑   ↗   →   ↘   ↓   ↙

Knock-knock.
  Who's there?
Agatha.
  Agatha who?
Agatha blues when it rains.

Knock-knock.
  Who's there?
Fletcher.
  Fletcher who?
Fletcher smile be your umbrella.

  ↑   ↗   →   ↘   ↓   ↙

Knock-knock.
Who's there?
A herd.
A herd who?
A herd you were home so I came over.

Knock-knock.
　Who's there?
Aida.
　Aida who?
Aida when I'm hungry and drink when I'm dry.

♠　　♟　　➡　　♞　　⬇　　♝

Knock-knock.
  Who's there?
Aisle.
  Aisle who?
Aisle be seeing you.

Knock-knock.
  Who's there?
Alaska.
  Alaska who?
Alaska questions around here.

Knock-knock.
  Who's there?
Albee.
  Albee who?
Albee a monkey's uncle.

Knock-knock.
  Who's there?
Alby
  Alby who?
Alby glad when school is over.

Knock-knock.
  Who's there?
Ida.
  Ida who?
Ida rather be playing outside.

Knock-knock.
  Who's there?
Alex.
  Alex who?
Alex New York in June.

  Knock-knock.
    Who's there?
House.
    House who?
House about you?

  ✦   ↗   ➡   ◤   ⬇   ◣

Knock-knock.
  Who's there?
Alf.
  Alf who?
Alf a loaf is better than none.

  ✦   ↗   ➡   ◤   ⬇   ◣

Knock-knock.
  Who's there?
Alfie.
  Alfie who?
Alfie you later.

    ▲   ▼   ▪

Knock-knock.
  Who's there?
Algae.
  Algae who?
Algae you in my
dreams.

Knock-knock.
  Who's
there?
Ollie.
  Ollie who?
"Ollie do is dream of you."

▲   ▩   ▶   ▪   ▼   ▪

Knock-knock.
  Who's there?
Ali.
  Ali who?
"Ali want is a room somewhere."

♠ ↗ ➡ ↘ ⬇ ↙

Knock-knock.
  Who's there?
Alibi.
  Alibi who?
Alibi you anything you want.

♠ ↗ ➡ ↘ ⬇ ↙

Knock-knock.
  Who's there?
Alice.
  Alice who?
Alice forgiven. Please come home.

♠ ↗ ➡ ↘ ⬇ ↙

Knock-knock.
  Who's there?
Alice.
  Alice who?
Alice fair in love and war.

  Knock-knock.
    Who's there?
  Annie.
    Annie who?
  Annie thing goes.

Knock-knock.
  Who's there?
Alison.
  Alison who?
Alison Wonderland is a great book.

✦　　✺　　➡　　✺　　⬇　　✺

Knock-knock.
  Who's there?
Alma.
  Alma who?
Alma bags are packed, I'm ready to go.

✦　　✺　　➡　　✺　　⬇　　✺

Knock-knock.
  Who's there?
Almond.
  Almond who?
"Almond love with a wonderful guy."

✦　　✺　　➡　　✺　　⬇　　✺

Knock-knock.
  Who's there?
Alpaca.
  Alpaca who?
Alpaca mean punch so don't mess with me.

↑   ↗   →   ↘   ↓   ↙

Knock-knock.
  Who's there?
Alpha.
  Alpha who?
Alpha crying out loud.

♠   ⟐   ➡   ⬛   ⬇   ◤

Knock-knock.
  Who's there?
Amahl.
  Amahl who?
Amahl yours.

♠   ⟐   ➡   ⬛   ⬇   ◤

Knock-knock.
  Who's there?
A Mayan.
  A Mayan who?
A Mayan the way?

♠   ⟐   ➡   ⬛   ⬇   ◤

Knock-knock.
Who's there?
Amish.
Amish who?
Amish is as good as a mile.

↑　↗　→　↘　↓　↙

Knock-knock.
Who's there?
Ammonia.
Ammonia who?
"Ammonia bird
in a gilded
cage."

↑　↗　→　↘　↓　↙

Knock-knock.
 Who's there?
Amoeba.
 Amoeba who?
Amoeba wrong but I think you're wonderful.

Knock-knock.
 Who's there?
Amos.
 Amos who?
Amos behavin.

Knock-knock.
 Who's there?
Amy.
 Amy who?
Amy name is Alice, my husband's name is
Arthur.

Knock-knock.
  Who's there?
Anastasia.
  Anastasia who?
Anastasia wagon has four doors.

Knock-knock.
  Who's there?
Ancient.
  Ancient who?
Ancient going to open the door?

♦ ⬈ ➡ ⬔ ⬇ ⬂

Knock-knock.
  Who's there?
Andy.
  Andy who?
Andy angels sing.

♦ ⬈ ➡ ⬔ ⬇ ⬂

Knock-knock.
  Who's there?
A Nicholas.
  A Nicholas who?
A Nicholas not much money these days.

♦ ⬈ ➡ ⬔ ⬇ ⬂

Knock-knock.
  Who's there?
Anita Baker.
  Anita Baker who?
Anita Baker for the party.

♠ ♜ ➡ ♟ ⬇ ♞

Knock-knock.
  Who's there?
Anna.
  Anna who?
Anna partridge in a pear tree.

♠   ↗   ➡   ◣   ⬇   ◤

Knock-knock.
  Who's there?
Annapolis.
  Annapolis who?
Annapolis is a fruit like a pear.

♠   ↗   ➡   ◣   ⬇   ◤

Knock-knock.
  Who's there?
Annette.
  Annette who?
Annette works where I find my favorite
TV show.

♠   ↗   ➡   ◣   ⬇   ◤

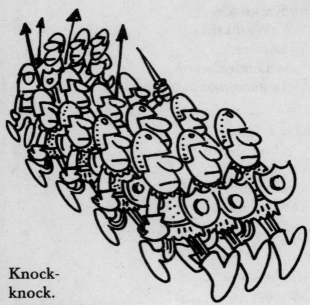

Knock-
knock.
   Who's there?
Anwar.
   Anwar who?
"Anwar Christian soldiers..."

Knock-knock.
  Who's there?
Lettuce.
  Lettuce who?
Lettuce pray.

✦   ✈   ➡   ◤   ⬇   ◣

Knock-knock.
  Who's there?
Aorta.
  Aorta who?
Aorta be in pictures.

Knock-knock.
  Who's there?
Snow.
  Snow who?
"Snow business like show business."

✦   ✈   ➡   ◤   ⬇   ◣

Knock-knock.
  Who's there?
Archie.
  Archie who?
Archie I was going to surprise you.

♠   ↗   ➡   ♟   ⬇   ◄

Knock-knock.
  Who's there?
Area.
  Area who?
Area there?

♠   ↗   ➡   ♟   ⬇   ◄

Knock-knock.
  Who's there?
Argo.
  Argo who?
Argo home, your mother is calling you.

♠   ↗   ➡   ♟   ⬇   ◄

Knock-knock.
   Who's there?
Aria.
   Aria who?
Aria ready for this?

Knock-knock.
   Who's there?
Arkansas.
   Arkansas who?
Arkansas more wood with my new chain saw.

Knock-knock.
  Who's there?
Armageddon.
  Armageddon who?
Armageddon ready for the last roundup.

  Knock-knock.
    Who's there?
  Barry.
    Barry who?
  "Barry me not on the lone prairie."

  ♠   ♜   ➡   ♟   ⬇   ♞

Knock-knock.
  Who's there?
Armando.
  Armando who?
"Armando road again."

Knock-knock.
  Who's there?
Olive.
  Olive who?
"Olive to go a-wandering."

♦ ⬕ ➡ ⬔ ⬇ ◤

Knock-knock.
  Who's there?
Armenia.
  Armenia who?
Armenia no harm.

↑ ↗ → ↘ ↓ ↙

Knock-knock.
  Who's there?
Asia.
  Asia who?
Asia is or Asia ain't my baby?

  Knock-knock.
    Who's there?
  Wanda.
    Wanda who?
  Wanda be my valentine?

✦　　✴　　➤　　◀　　⬇　　◣

Knock-knock.
  Who's there?
Asthma.
  Asthma who?
Asthma no questions and I'll tell you no
lies.

  ✦　　✴　　➤　　◀　　⬇　　◣

Knock-knock.
  Who's there?
Atom.
  Atom who?
Atom 'n Eve.

　✦　　🡵　　➡　　🡶　　⬇　　🡶

Knock-knock.
  Who's there?
Atwood.
  Atwood who?
Atwood only take a second.

　✦　　🡵　　➡　　🡶　　⬇　　🡶

Knock-knock.
  Who's there?
Augusta.
  Augusta who?
Augusta wind blew my hat off.

　✦　　🡵　　➡　　🡶　　⬇　　🡶

Knock-knock.
  Who's there?
Aurora.
  Aurora who?
Aurora is what a lion is.

↑ ↖ → ↘ ↓ ↙

Knock-knock.
  Who's there?
Author.
  Author who?
Author any more at home like you?

↑ ↖ → ↘ ↓ ↙

Knock-knock.
  Who's there?
Auto.
  Auto who?
Auto know but I forgot.

Knock-knock.
  Who's there?
Don.
  Don who?
Don know. I've got
amnesia.

Knock-knock.
  Who's there?
Yoda.
  Yoda who?
Yoda most forgetful person I know.

    ↟   ↗   ➡   ↘   ↓   ↙

Knock-knock.
  Who's there?
Avenue.
  Avenue who?
Avenue baby sister.

    ↟   ↗   ➡   ↘   ↓   ↙

Knock-knock.
  Who's there?
Avenue.
  Avenue who?
Avenue knocked on this door before?

    ↟   ↗   ➡   ↘   ↓   ↙

Knock-knock.
  Who's there?
Avery.
  Avery who?
Avery dog has his day.

Knock-knock.
Who's there?
Avoid.
Avoid who?
Avoid this joke before.

Knock-knock.
Who's there?
Award.
Award who?
Award to the wise is sufficient.

Knock-knock.
Who's there?
Aware.
Aware who?
"Aware, aware has my little dog gone?"

Knock-knock.

Who's there?

Awesome.

Awesome who?

Awesome of these jokes supposed to be funny?

Knock-knock.
  Who's there?
Awful.
  Awful who?
Awful one and one for all.

♠ ⬈ ➡ ⬊ ⬇ ⬉

Knock-knock.
  Who's there?
Axe.
  Axe who?
Axe your mother if you can come out and play.

Knock-knock.
  Who's there?
Kenya.
  Kenya who?
Kenya come out and play.

♠ ⬈ ➡ ⬊ ⬇ ⬉

Knock-knock.
  Who's there?
Bach.
  Bach who?
Bach to the drawing board.

♠   ♣   ➡   ♦   ♥   ⬋

Knock-knock.
  Who's there?
Bacon.
  Bacon who?
Bacon your pardon.

♠ ♞ ➡ ♞ ⬇ ♞

Knock-knock.
  Who's there?
Baloney.
  Baloney who?
Baloney God can make a tree.

♠ ♞ ➡ ♞ ⬇ ♞

Knock-knock.
  Who's there?
Barber.
  Barber who?
Barber Streisand.

♠ ♞ ➡ ♞ ⬇ ♞

Knock-knock.
  Who's there?
Barbie.
  Barbie who?
Barbie-cue is burning.

♠ ♯ ➡ ⬏ ⬇ ⬐

Knock-knock.
  Who's there?
Barry.
  Barry who?
Barry the hatchet.

♠ ♯ ➡ ⬏ ⬇ ⬐

Knock-knock.
  Who's there?
Barton.
  Barton who?
Barton down the hatches.

✦   ⚡   ➡   ⚡   ⬇   ✦

Knock-knock.
  Who's there?
Bat.
  Bat who?
Bat you can't guess.

✦   ⚡   ➡   ⚡   ⬇   ✦

Knock-knock.
  Who's there?
Bay.
  Bay who?
"Bay-be face. You've got the cutest little baby face."

✦   ⚡   ➡   ⚡   ⬇   ✦

Knock-knock.
   Who's there?
Bayou.
   Bayou who?
Bayou a soda if you lend me a dollar.

✦   ✦   ✦   ✦   ✦   ✦

Knock-knock.
   Who's there?
Bea.
   Bea who?
Bea good sport and open the door.

✦   ✦   ✦   ✦   ✦   ✦

Knock-knock.
  Who's there?
Beach.
  Beach who?

Knock-knock.
  Who's there?
Beach.
  Beach who?

Knock-knock.
  Who's there?
Beach.
  Beach who?

  Knock-knock.
    Who's there?
  Shore.
    Shore who?
  Shore glad I didn't say beach again.

♠ ▨ ➡ ▧ ⬇ ◪

49

Knock-knock.
  Who's there?
Beans.
  Beans who?
Beans so long I hardly recognize you.

Knock-knock.
  Who's there?
Bear.
  Bear who?
Bear are you, it's dark outside.

Knock-knock.
  Who's there?
Beater.
  Beater who?
Beater round the bush.

Knock-knock.
  Who's there?
Beats.
  Beats who?
Beats me, I forgot my name.

Knock-knock.
  Who's there?
Beef.
  Beef who?
Beef-fore I tell you, let me in.

Knock-knock.
  Who's there?
Believing.
  Believing who?
Believing if you don't open the door.

Knock-knock.
  Who's there?
Ben.
  Ben who?
Ben knocking so long my hand hurts.

Knock-knock.
  Who's there?
Ben Hur.
  Ben Hur who?
Ben Hur for 10 minutes and nobody
showed up.

Knock-knock.
  Who's there?
Betty.
  Betty who?
Betty gets sore knuckles from all that
knocking.

✦　　♞　　➡　　♟　　⬇　　♜

Knock-knock.
  Who's there?
Bess.
  Bess who?
Bess of luck.

✦　　♞　　➡　　♟　　⬇　　♜

Knock-knock.

Who's there?

Beta watch.

Beta watch who?

"Beta watch out, beta not cry, beta not pout, I'm telling you why, Santa Claus is coming to town."

Knock-knock.
  Who's there?
Beth.
  Beth who?
Beth you can't guess.

▲   ◸   ➜   ◢   ⬇   ◣

Knock-knock.
  Who's there?
Bias.
  Bias who?
Bias many as you need.

▲   ◸   ➜   ◢   ⬇   ◣

Knock-knock.
  Who's there?
Bifocal.
  Bifocal who?
Bifocal built for two.

▲   ◸   ➜   ◢   ⬇   ◣

Knock-knock.
  Who's there?
Big Horse.
  Big Horse who?
"Big Horse of you there's a song in my heart."

♠ ♜ ➡ ♟ ⬇ ♞

Knock-knock.
Who's there?
Bjorn.
Bjorn who?
"Bjorn free, as free as the wind blows."

♦ ⚐ ➨ ◤ ⬇ ◣

Knock-knock.
Who's there?
Black Panther.
Black Panther who?
Black Panther in the wash so I wore my brown ones.

♦ ⚐ ➨ ◤ ⬇ ◣

Knock-knock.
Who's there?
Bob.
Bob who?
"Bob, Bob, black sheep, have you any wool?"

♦ ⚐ ➨ ◤ ⬇ ◣

Knock-knock.
  Who's there?
Boo-hoo.
  Boo-hoo who?
Stop it, you're breaking my heart.

Knock-knock.
  Who's there?
Boris.
  Boris who?
Boris to death, why don't you?

↑   →   ↓

Knock-knock.
  Who's there?
Boycott.
  Boycott who?
Boycott his jeans on the fence.

↑   →   ↓

Knock-knock.
  Who's there?
Boyd.
  Boyd who?
Boyd, did I make a mistake.

↑   →   ↓

Knock-knock.
   Who's there?
Brahms.
   Brahms who?
"Brahms bursting in air."

Knock-knock.
   Who's there?
Braise.
   Braise who?
"Braise the Lord and pass the ammunition."

Knock-knock.
  Who's there?
Brighton.
  Brighton who?
Brighton early.

Knock-knock.
  Who's there?
Budget.
  Budget who?
If you budget, it will go through the door
easier.

Knock-knock.
  Who's there?
Burden.
  Burden who?
"Burden the hand is worth two in the
bush."

Knock-knock.
　Who's there?
Burton.
　Burton who?
"Burton up your overcoat."

♠　　♬　　➡　　♘　　⬇　　♜

Knock-knock.
　Who's there?
Buster.
　Buster who?
Buster gut.

♠　　♬　　➡　　♘　　⬇　　♜

Knock-knock.
　Who's there?
Butter.
　Butter who?
Butter late than never.

♠　　♬　　➡　　♘　　⬇　　♜

Knock-knock.
  Who's there?
Butternut.
  Butternut who?
Butternut try to pick up a skunk.

✦　　◀　　➡　　◥　　⬇　　◤

Knock-knock.
  Who's there?
Bwana.
  Bwana who?
"Bwana hold your hand."

✦　　◀　　➡　　◥　　⬇　　◤

Knock-knock.
  Who's there?
Cadillac.
  Cadillac who?
Cadillac mad if you step on its tail.

♠   ✒   ➡   ✖   ⬇   ✘

Knock-knock.
  Who's there?
Cairo.
  Cairo who?
Cairo the boat?

Knock-knock.
  Who's there?
Calcutta.
  Calcutta who?
Calcutta cut a hole in the paper.

Knock-knock.
  Who's there?
Cameron.
  Cameron who?
Cameron film are ready, say cheese.

Knock-knock.
  Who's there?
Camphor.
  Camphor who?
Camphor the life of me remember your name.

↑ ↗ → ↘ ↓ ↙

Knock-knock.
  Who's there?
Canape.
  Canape who?
Canape you by check?

♠   ↗   ➡   ↘   ⬇   ↙

Knock-knock.
  Who's there?
Candice.
  Candice who?
Candice be the last joke?

♠   ↗   ➡   ↘   ⬇   ↙

Knock-knock.
  Who's there?
Candidate.
  Candidate who?
Candidate be changed to Friday?

♠   ↗   ➡   ↘   ⬇   ↙

Knock-knock.
  Who's there?
Cantina.
  Cantina who?
Cantina have a cookie?

Knock-knock.
  Who's there?
Cargo.
  Cargo who?
Cargo, "Vroom,
vroom."

Knock-knock.
  Who's there?
Carlotta.
  Carlotta who?
Carlotta trouble when it breaks down.

♦   ⚐   ➡   ⚑   ⬇   ⬉

Knock-knock.
  Who's there?
Carmen.
  Carmen who?
"Carmen in on a wing and a prayer."

♦   ⚐   ➡   ⚑   ⬇   ⬉

Knock-knock.
  Who's there?
Carrie.
  Carrie who?
"Carrie me back to old Virginny."

♦   ⚐   ➡   ⚑   ⬇   ⬉

Knock-knock.
  Who's there?
Carrier.
  Carrier who?
Carrier over the threshold.

↑　↗　→　↘　↓　↙

Knock-knock.
  Who's there?
Cash.
  Cash who?
Got any nuts?

↑　↗　→　↘　↓　↙

Knock-knock.
  Who's there?
Cashew.
  Cashew who?
Cashew goofing off again and you're fired.

↑　↗　→　↘　↓　↙

Knock-knock.

  Who's there?

Cashews.

  Cashews who?

Cashews don't fit and my feet are killing me.

Knock-knock.
  Who's there?
Castor.
  Castor who?
Castor bread upon the water.

Knock-knock.
  Who's there?
Catch.
  Catch who?
Bless you.

Knock-knock.
  Who's there?
Catkin.
  Catkin who?
Catkin see in the dark.

Knock-knock.
Who's there?
Cattle.
Cattle who?
Cattle purr if you pet it.

Knock-knock.
  Who's there?
Cedar.
  Cedar who?
"Cedar pyramids along the Nile."

↑   ↗   →   ↘   ↓   ↙

Knock-knock.
  Who's there?
Celeste.
  Celeste who?
Celeste time I'm going to lend you money.

↑   ↗   →   ↘   ↓   ↙

Knock-knock.
  Who's there?
Celia.
  Celia who?
Celia envelope before you mail it.

♠ ♜ ➡ ♟ ⬇ ◣

Knock-knock.
  Who's there?
Cello.
  Cello who?
"Cello acquaintance be forgot."

♠ ♜ ➡ ♟ ⬇ ◣

Knock-knock.
  Who's there?
Censure.
  Censure who?
Censure so smart, why aren't you rich?

♠ ♜ ➡ ♟ ⬇ ◣

Knock-knock.
    Who's there?
Ceylon.
    Ceylon who?
"Ceylon," Columbus told his men.

⬆ ⚔ ➡ ⚔ ⬇ ⚔

Knock-knock.
  Who's there?
Chair.
  Chair who?
Chair your sandwich, I'm hungry.

Knock-knock.
  Who's there?
Champ.
  Champ who?
Champ who and a haircut, six bucks.

Knock-knock.
  Who's there?
Charlotte.
  Charlotte who?
Charlotte of mosquitoes out tonight.

Knock-knock.
  Who's there?
Cheese.
  Cheese who?
Cheese funny that way.

Knock-knock.
  Who's there?
Chelsea.
  Chelsea who?
Chelsea you in my dreams.

Knock-knock.
Who's there?
Chemise.
Chemise who?
Chemise me when I'm gone?

↑ ↗ → ↘ ↓ ↙

Knock-knock.
Who's there?
Chess.
Chess who?
Chess one of those things.

↑ ↗ → ↘ ↓ ↙

Knock-knock.
Who's there?
Chester.
Chester who?
Chester minute and you'll find out.

↑ ↗ → ↘ ↓ ↙

Knock-knock.
  Who's there?
Chicken.
  Chicken who?
Chicken up on you.

Knock-knock.
  Who's there?
Ivan.
  Ivan who?
Ivan watching you.

Knock-knock.
  Who's there?
Cicero.
  Cicero who?
Cicero row I sit in?

♠   ♯   ➡   ♯   ⬇   ☛

Knock-knock.
  Who's there?
Cinder.
  Cinder who?
Cinder top drawer with your socks.

♠   ♯   ➡   ♯   ⬇   ☛

Knock-knock.
  Who's there?
Cindy.
  Cindy who?
"Cindy cool, cool, cool of the evening."

♠   ♯   ➡   ♯   ⬇   ☛

Knock-knock.
  Who's there?
Claude.
  Claude who?
Claude his way to the top.

↑   ➚   →   ➛   ↓   ➝

Knock-knock.
  Who's there?
Clothes.
  Clothes who?
Clothes the door.

↑   ➚   →   ➛   ↓   ➝

Knock-knock.
  Who's there?
Colleen.
  Colleen who?
Colleen up your room.

↑   ➚   →   ➛   ↓   ➝

Knock-knock.
  Who's there?
Collie.
  Collie who?
"Collie-fornia here I come."

Knock-knock.
  Who's there?
Comb.
  Comb who?
Comb over to my house.

Knock-knock.
  Who's there?
Congo.
  Congo who?
"Congo on, everything I have is gone,
stormy weather..."

↑ ↗ → ↘ ↓ ↙

Knock-knock.
  Who's there?
Consumption.
  Consumption who?
Consumption be done about these knock-knock jokes?

Knock-knock.
  Who's there?
Armageddon.
  Armageddon who?
Armageddon tired of these knock-knock jokes.

♠   ♞   ♦   ♜   ♥   ♝

Knock-knock.
  Who's there?
Could she.
  Could she who?
Could she, koochy she coo.

♠   ♞   ♦   ♜   ♥   ♝

Knock-knock.
  Who's there?
Creature.
  Creature who?
Creature friends with more respect.

  Knock-knock.
    Who's there?
  Voodoo.
    Voodoo who?
  Voodoo you think you are?

↑   ↗   →   ↘   ↓   ↙

Knock-knock.
  Who's there?
Cumin.
  Cumin who?
Cumin get it!

↑   ↗   →   ↘   ↓   ↙

Knock-knock.
 Who's there?
Custer.
 Custer who?
Custer pretty penny.

Knock-knock.
  Who's there?
Dakar.
  Dakar who?
Dakar is broken, I had to walk.

Knock-knock.
  Who's there?
Dallas.
  Dallas who?
Dallas in Wonderland.

      ♠   ⏏   ➡   ⬐   ⬇   ◄

Knock-knock.
  Who's there?
Damascus.
  Damascus who?
Damascus what you wear on Halloween.

      ♠   ⏏   ➡   ⬐   ⬇   ◄

Knock-knock.
  Who's there?
Dandelion.
  Dandelion who?
Isn't it Dandelion around all day doing
nothing?

      ♠   ⏏   ➡   ⬐   ⬇   ◄

Knock-knock.
   Who's there?
Darren.
   Darren who?
"Darren young man on the flying trapeze."

   ✦   ⤢   ➡   ⬃   ⬇   ⬂

Knock-knock.
   Who's there?
Datsun.
   Datsun who?
"Datsun will come out tomorrow."

   Knock-knock.
      Who's there?
Icon.
   Icon who?
"Icon see clearly now the rain has
gone."

   ✦   ⤢   ➡   ⬃   ⬇   ⬂

Knock-knock.
    Who's there?
Datsun.
    Datsun who?
Datsun of mine is spoiled.

Knock-knock.
  Who's there?
Deep Ends.
  Deep Ends who?
"All Deep Ends on you."

♠   ♠   ➡   ♠   ⬇   ♠

Knock-knock.
  Who's there?
Defeat, defense and detail.
  Defeat, defense and detail who?
Defeat of the dog jumped over defense
before detail.

♠   ♠   ➡   ♠   ⬇   ♠

Knock-knock.
  Who's there?
Defy.
  Defy who?
"Defy knew you were coming I'd have
baked a cake."

♠   ♠   ➡   ♠   ⬇   ♠

Knock-knock.
  Who's there?
Delaware.
  Delaware who?
Delaware your new dress to the party.

Knock-knock.
  Who's there?
Auto.
  Auto who?
Auto meet me when I'm dressed up.

Knock-knock.
  Who's there?
Déjà.
  Déjà who?
No, déjà vu.

♠ ↗ ➡ ◣ ⬇ ◤

Knock-knock.
  Who's there?
Deli.
  Deli who?
Deli-catessen.

♠ ↗ ➡ ◣ ⬇ ◤

Knock-knock.
  Who's there?
Delia.
  Delia who?
Delia cards.

♠ ↗ ➡ ◣ ⬇ ◤

Knock-knock.
　Who's there?
Delight.
　Delight who?
"Delight of the silvery moon."

⬆ ⬈ ➡ ⬊ ⬇ ⬋

Knock-knock.
  Who's there?
Denise.
  Denise who?
Denise, de sister of de nephew.

♦　　◪　　➡　　◪　　⬇　　◪

Knock-knock.
  Who's there?
Despair.
  Despair who?
Despair tire is flat.

♦　　◪　　➡　　◪　　⬇　　◪

Knock-knock.
  Who's there?
Detour.
  Detour who?
Detour is over, you're on your own.

♦　　◪　　➡　　◪　　⬇　　◪

Knock-knock.
  Who's there?
Dewey.
  Dewey who?
Dewey have to go on meeting like this?

Knock-knock.
  Who's there?
Diesel.
  Diesel who?
Diesel be over before you know it.

Knock-knock.
  Who's there?
Dishes.
  Dishes who?
Dishes the F.B.I. Open up!

Knock-knock.
  Who's there?
Frieda.
  Frieda who?
Frieda hostages!

Knock-knock.
  Who's there?
Disguise.
  Disguise who?
Disguise the limit.

Knock-knock.
  Who's there?
Dismay.
  Dismay who?
Dismay be my last knock-knock joke.

Knock-knock.
  Who's there?
Domino.
  Domino who?
"Domino cow hand from the Rio Grande."

Knock-knock.
  Who's there?
Don.
  Don who?
"Don cry for me, Argentina."

   ↑   ↗   →   ↘   ↓   ↙

Knock-knock.
  Who's there?
Donahue.
  Donahue who?
Donahue yell at me.

   ↑   ↗   →   ↘   ↓   ↙

Knock-knock.
  Who's there?
Donkey.
  Donkey who?
Donkey-ote.

   ↑   ↗   →   ↘   ↓   ↙

Knock-knock.
  Who's there?
Donna.
  Donna who?
"Donna let the stars get in your eyes."

✦ ⬈ ➡ ⬎ ⬇ ⬊

Knock-knock.
  Who's there?
The doorbell repairman.

✦ ⬈ ➡ ⬎ ⬇ ⬊

Knock-knock.
  Who's there?
Doris.
  Doris who?
"Doris nothing like a dame."

Knock-knock.
  Who's there?
Dots.
  Dots who?
Dots for me to know and you to find out.

Knock-knock.
  Who's there?
Doug.
  Doug who?
Doug a hole on your doorstep.

Knock-knock.
  Who's there?
Doughnut.
  Doughnut who?
"Doughnut make my brown eyes blue."

Knock-knock.
  Who's there?
Dozen.
  Dozen who?
Dozen anybody want to let me in?

♦ ⬈ ➡ ◪ ⬇ ◧

Knock-knock.
  Who's there?
Dresden.
  Dresden who?
Dresden your Sunday best.

Knock-knock.
  Who's there?
Dozen.
  Dozen who?
Dozen she look nice.

♦ ⬈ ➡ ◪ ⬇ ◧

Knock-knock.
   Who's there?
Duet.
   Duet who?
Duet again.

Knock-knock.
   Who's there?
Duluth.
   Duluth who?
Duluth tooth will get you a quarter.

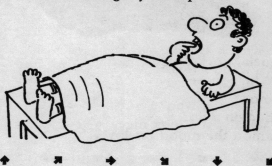

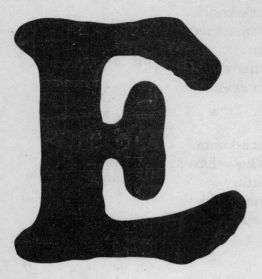

Knock-knock.
  Who's there?
Eamon.
  Eamon who?
"Eamon the mood for love."

Knock-knock.
  Who's there?
Earle.
  Earle who?
"Earle I want for Christmas is my two
front teeth."

↑ ↗ → ↘ ↓ ↙

Knock-knock.
  Who's there?
Eclipse.
  Eclipse who?
Eclipse my hair too close, that barber.

↑ ↗ → ↘ ↓ ↙

Knock-knock.
  Who's there?
Edsel.
  Edsel who?
Edsel there is, there ain't no more.

↑ ↗ → ↘ ↓ ↙

Knock-knock.

   Who's there?

Eel.

   Eel who?

Eel feel better in the morning.

Knock-knock.
  Who's there?
Effervescent.
  Effervescent who?
Effervescent for you, I'd be done already.

♠ ⚐ ➡ ⚐ ⬇ ⚐

Knock-knock.
  Who's there?
Eiffel.
  Eiffel who?
Eiffel good. I knew I would.

♠ ⚐ ➡ ⚐ ⬇ ⚐

Knock-knock.
  Who's there?
Eliza.
  Eliza who?
Eliza lot, so watch your step.

♠ ⚐ ➡ ⚐ ⬇ ⚐

Knock-knock.
  Who's there?
Ellen.
  Ellen who?
Ellen you a dollar, but pay me back.

➜ ➜ ➜ ➜ ➜ ➜

Knock-knock.
  Who's there?
Emerson.
  Emerson who?
Emerson some nice shoes you have on.

  Knock-knock.
    Who's there?
Butternut.
    Butternut who?
Butternut let me in, I have mud on my
shoes.

➜ ➜ ➜ ➜ ➜ ➜

Knock-knock.
　Who's there?
Emile.
　Emile who?
Emile fit for a king.

♠　♣　➡　♦　♦　♦

Knock-knock.
  Who's there?
Emma.
  Emma who?
"Emma blue?"

Knock-knock.
  Who's there?
Lyle.
  Lyle who?
Lyle never smile again.

Knock-knock.
  Who's there?
Eskimo.
  Eskimo who?
Eskimo-ver for dinner.

♠   ♫   ➜   ✦   ⬇   ⬊

Knock-knock.
  Who's there?
Essay.
  Essay who?
Essay a little prayer for you.

♠   ♫   ➜   ✦   ⬇   ⬊

Knock-knock.
  Who's there?
Esther.
  Esther who?
Esther room for one more?

♠   ♫   ➜   ✦   ⬇   ⬊

Knock-knock.
  Who's there?
E.T.
  E.T. who?
E.T. your food before it gets cold.

⬆ ⬈ ➡ ⬊ ⬇ ⬋

Knock-knock.
  Who's there?
Eubie.
  Eubie who?
"Eubie long to me."

⬆ ⬈ ➡ ⬊ ⬇ ⬋

Knock-knock.
  Who's there?
Europe.
  Europe who?
Europe the creek without a paddle.

⬆ ⬈ ➡ ⬊ ⬇ ⬋

Knock-knock.
  Who's there?
Eva.
  Eva who?
Eva the worm will turn.

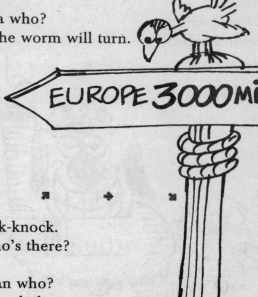

Knock-knock.
  Who's there?
Evan.
  Evan who?
Evan only knows.

Knock-knock.
  Who's there?
Event.
  Event who?
Event thataway.

Knock-knock.
  Who's there?
Eyesore.
  Eyesore who?
Eyesore that!

✦　　✺　　➜　　❯　　⬇　　❮

Knock-knock.
  Who's there?
Eyewash.
  Eyewash who?
"Eyewash you a Merry Christmas."

✦　　✺　　➜　　❯　　⬇　　❮

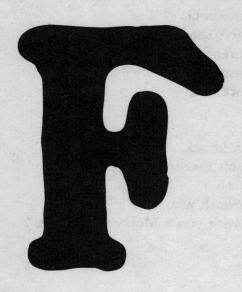

Knock-knock.
 Who's there?
Fabric.
 Fabric who?
Fabric hits you on the head, you see stars.

Knock-knock.
 Who's there?
Fairbanks.
 Fairbanks who?
Fairbanks pay interest.

♠   ⚑   ➡   ◀   ⬇   ◄

Knock-knock.
 Who's there?
Faith.
 Faith who?
Faith looks familiar.

♠   ⚑   ➡   ◀   ⬇   ◄

Knock-knock.
 Who's there?
Fantasy.
 Fantasy who?
Fantasy a movie last night.

♠   ⚑   ➡   ◀   ⬇   ◄

Knock-knock.
  Who's there?
Fangs.
  Fangs who?
"Fangs for the memories."

▲ ▲ ➢ ▲ ⬇ ▲

Knock-knock.
  Who's there?
Farm.
  Farm who?
Farm me to know and you to find out.

▲ ▲ ➢ ▲ ⬇ ▲

Knock-knock.
  Who's there?
Ferry.
  Ferry who?
"Ferry tales can come true."

Knock-knock.
 Who's there?
Wren.
 Wren who?
"Wren you wish upon a star."

Knock-knock.
  Who's there?
Psalm.
  Psalm who?
"Psalm day my prince will come."

   ✦   ⇗   ➡   ↘   ⬇   ◪

Knock-knock.
  Who's there?
Fido.
  Fido who?
Fido I have to wait out here?

Knock-knock.
  Who's there?
Venus
  Venus who?
Venus you going to open the door?

➤ ➤ ➤ ➤ ➤ ➤

Knock-knock.
  Who's there?
Fire engine.
  Fire engine who?
Fire engine one and prepare for blast off.

➤ ➤ ➤ ➤ ➤ ➤

Knock-knock.
  Who's there?
Flea.
  Flea who?
Flea blind mice.

➤ ➤ ➤ ➤ ➤ ➤

Knock-knock.
  Who's there?
Fletcher.
  Fletcher who?
Fletcher conscience be your guide.

✦ 🢔 ➡ 🢖 ⬇ 🢗

Knock-knock.
  Who's there?
Folder.
  Folder who?
Folder knows best.

✦ 🢔 ➡ 🢖 ⬇ 🢗

Knock-knock.
  Who's there?
Formosa.
  Formosa who?
Formosa my life I stand on your doorstep.

✦ 🢔 ➡ 🢖 ⬇ 🢗

Knock-knock.
  Who's there?
Forty.
  Forty who?
Forty life of me I can't remember.

Knock-knock.
  Who's there?
Foyer.
  Foyer who?
Foyer information it's your brother.

♠   ♪   ➡   ♞   ⬇   ♜

Knock-knock.
  Who's there?
Francis.
  Francis who?
Francis where people speak French.

Knock-knock.
  Who's there?
Celeste.
  Celeste who?
"Celeste time I saw Paris."

♠   ♪   ➡   ♞   ⬇   ♜

Knock-knock.
  Who's there?
Frasier.
  Frasier who?
Frasier never going to open the door.

Knock-knock.
  Who's there?
Frayda.
  Frayda who?
"Who's a Frayda the big, bad wolf?"

Knock-knock.
  Who's there?
Freddy.
  Freddy who?
Freddy when you are.

▲ △ ▶ ▷ ▼ ▽

Knock-knock.
  Who's there?
Freighter.
  Freighter who?
Freighter your own shadow.

▲ △ ▶ ▷ ▼ ▽

Knock-knock.
  Who's there?
Fresno.
  Fresno who?
Fresno genius, but I love him just the
same.

▲ △ ▶ ▷ ▼ ▽

Knock-knock.
  Who's there?
Frieda.
  Frieda who?
Frieda cold and starve a fever.

Knock-knock.
  Who's there?
Ghana.
  Ghana who?
Ghana be famous someday.

Knock-knock.
  Who's there?
Gibbon.
  Gibbon who?
Gibbon an inch and he'll take a mile.

Knock-knock.
  Who's there?
Gladys.
  Gladys who?
Gladys Friday.

  Knock-knock.
    Who's there?
Orange.
    Orange who?
Orange you glad school's out?

Knock-knock.
  Who's there?
Gopher.
  Gopher who?
Gopher your gun, Marshal.

Knock-knock.
  Who's there?
Pasta.
  Pasta who?
Pasta la vista, baby.

✦   ✖   ➡   ✖   ⬇   ✖

Knock-knock.
  Who's there?
Gopher.
  Gopher who?
Gopher a long walk on a short pier.

✦   ✖   ➡   ✖   ⬇   ✖

Knock-knock.
  Who's there?
Gomez.
  Gomez who?
Gomez around with someone else. I'm
busy.

Knock-knock.
  Who's there?
Gorilla.
  Gorilla who?
Gorilla my dreams!

♠   ✹   ➡   ✹   ⬇   ✹

Knock-knock.
  Who's there?
Grover.
  Grover who?
Grover to the fridge and get me a soda.

Knock-knock.
  Who's there?
Kansas.
  Kansas who?
Kansas better than bottles for soda.

♠   ✹   ➡   ✹   ⬇   ✹

Knock-knock.
  Who's there?
Gruel.
  Gruel who?
"Gruel days, gruel days, dear old golden
gruel days."

↑ ⬈ → ⬊ ↓ ⬋

Knock-knock.
  Who's there?
Gull.
  Gull who?
"Gull of my dreams."

↑ ⬈ → ⬊ ↓ ⬋

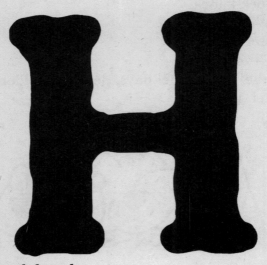

Knock-knock.
   Who's there?
Habit.
   Habit who?
Habit your way.

Knock-knock.
  Who's there?
Haddock.
  Haddock who?
Haddock is killing me, got an aspirin?

  Knock-knock.
    Who's there?
Thistle.
    Thistle who?
Thistle make you feel better.

♠   ↗   ➡   ⬀   ⬇   ↙

Knock-knock.
  Who's there?
Hammond.
  Hammond who?
Hammond cheese on rye, please.

♠   ↗   ➡   ⬀   ⬇   ↙

Knock-knock.
  Who's there?
Hank.
  Hank who?
Hank E. Chief.

✦　☈　➡　☋　⬇　☚

Knock-knock.
  Who's there?
Hannah.
  Hannah who?
Hannah me some potato chips.

✦　☈　➡　☋　⬇　☚

Knock-knock.
  Who's there?
Harlow.
  Harlow who?
"Harlow Dolly, well Harlow Dolly."

✦　☈　➡　☋　⬇　☚

Knock-knock.
  Who's there?
Harmon.
  Harmon who?
"Harmon love with a wonderful guy."

Knock-knock.
  Who's there?
Harness.
  Harness who?
Harness to goodness.

140

Knock-knock.
  Who's there?
Harry.
  Harry who?
Harry up, I'm starving.

  Knock-knock.
    Who's there?
  Abbot.
    Abbot who?
  Abbot time we eat, isn't it?

Knock-knock.
  Who's there?
Dewey.
  Dewey who?
Dewey have to wait so long to eat?

Knock-knock.
  Who's there?
Harvey.
  Harvey who?
Harvey having fun or what?

  Knock-knock.
    Who's there?
  Ali.
    Ali who?
  "Ali round the world people are dancing
  in the streets."

  ⬆   ⬈   ➡   ⬊   ⬇   ⬋

Knock-knock.
  Who's there?
Hassan.
  Hassan who?
Hassan anybody here seen Kelly?

  ⬆   ⬈   ➡   ⬊   ⬇   ⬋

Knock-knock.
  Who's there?
Havana.
  Havana who?
Havana go home.

Knock-knock.
  Who's there?
Hawaii.
  Hawaii who?
I'm fine. How are you?

Knock-knock.

  Who's there?

Heaven.

  Heaven who?

Heaven a wonderful time, wish you were here.

⬆ ⬈ ➡ ⬊ ⬇ ⬋

144

Knock-knock.
  Who's there?
Heidi.
  Heidi who?
Heidi ho.

✦ ✦ ✦ ✦ ✦ ✦

Knock-knock.
  Who's there?
Hence.
  Hence who?
Hence lay eggs.

✦ ✦ ✦ ✦ ✦ ✦

Knock-knock.
  Who's there?
Henny.
  Henny who?
Henny port in a storm.

✦ ✦ ✦ ✦ ✦ ✦

Knock-knock.
  Who's there?
Henrietta.
  Henrietta who?
Henrietta banana split.

⬆ ↗ ➡ ↘ ⬇ ↙

Knock-knock.
  Who's there?
Hester.
  Hester who?
Hester anything I can do for you?

⬆ ↗ ➡ ↘ ⬇ ↙

Knock-knock.
  Who's there?
Hive.
  Hive who?
Hive a crush on you.

⬆ ↗ ➡ ↘ ⬇ ↙

Knock-knock.
  Who's there?
Hominy.
  Hominy who?
Hominy people live here?

Knock-knock.
  Who's there?
Honeybee.
  Honeybee who?
Honeybee nice and open the door.

↑　　↗　　→　　↘　　↓　　↙

Knock-knock.
  Who's there?
Honeydew.
  Honeydew who?
Honeydew you love me?

↑　　↗　　→　　↘　　↓　　↙

Knock-knock.
  Who's there?
Hoosier.
  Hoosier who?
"Hoosier afraid of the big, bad wolf?"

↑　　↗　　→　　↘　　↓　　↙

Knock-knock.
　Who's there?
Hoosier.
　Hoosier who?
Hoosier favorite person in the whole world?

Knock-knock.
　Who's there?
Hootie.
　Hootie who?
Hootie think you're talking to?

✦　　ⵣ　　➡　　⬏　　⬇　　↙

Knock-knock.
　Who's there?
Hopi.
　Hopi who?
Hopi New Year!

✦　　ⵣ　　➡　　⬏　　⬇　　↙

Knock-knock.
　Who's there?
House.
　House who?
House business?

✦　　ⵣ　　➡　　⬏　　⬇　　↙

Knock-knock.
   Who's there?
Howard.
   Howard who?
Howard I know?

Knock-knock.
  Who's there?
Howard Hughes.
  Howard Hughes who?
Howard Hughes like a piece of candy?

Knock-knock.
  Who's there?
Howdy.
  Howdy who?
Howdy you stand all these knock-knock
jokes?

Knock-knock.
  Who's there?
Hugh.
  Hugh who?
Hugh must be sick and tired of these
knock-knock jokes.

Knock-knock.
  Who's there?
Howell.
  Howell who?
Howell done do you want your burger?

Knock-knock.
  Who's there?
Howl.
  Howl who?
Howl I get in if you don't open the door?

Knock-knock.
  Who's there?
Howdy.
  Howdy who?
Howdy I get in here?

Knock-knock.
  Who's there?
Celeste.
  Celeste who?
Celeste chance to open the door.

↑   ↪   →   ↴   ↓   ↲

Knock-knock.
  Who's there?
Hugo.
  Hugo who?
Hugo first, I'll follow.

↑   ↪   →   ↴   ↓   ↲

Knock-knock.

Who's there?

Humus.

Humus who?

"Humus have been a beautiful baby."

Knock-knock.
  Who's there?
Huron.
  Huron who?
Huron the hot seat now.

Knock-knock.
  Who's there?
Dinosaur.
  Dinosaur who?
Dinosaur because his mother spanked him.

Knock-knock.
 Who's there?
Hyena.
 Hyena who?
Hyena tree sat an owl.

   ✦   ➹   ➡   ➘   ⬇   ↙

Knock-knock.
 Who's there?
Hyman.
 Hyman who?
Hyman a terrible hurry.

   ✦   ➹   ➡   ➘   ⬇   ↙

Knock-knock.
  Who's there?
I am.
  I am who?
You mean you don't know me either?

Knock-knock.
   Who's there?
Icon.
   Icon who?
"Icon get it for you wholesale."

Knock-knock.
   Who's there?
Ida.
   Ida who?
Ida like to shake your hand.

Knock-knock.
   Who's there?
Idaho.
   Idaho who?
Idaho-ped I'd get out of here sooner.

Knock-knock.
  Who's there?
Ida Mann.
  Ida Mann who?
Ida Mann you open the door.

✦   ⚘   ➡   🔄   ⬇   🔙

Knock-knock.
  Who's there?
Iguana.
  Iguana who?
Iguana go home.

✦   ⚘   ➡   🔄   ⬇   🔙

Knock-knock.
  Who's there?
Imus.
  Imus who?
Imus be going.

Knock-knock.
  Who's there?
Lyle.
  Lyle who?
Lyle be seeing you.

Knock-knock.
　Who's there?
Iona.
　Iona who?
Iona new bike.

Knock-knock.
  Who's there?
Iowa.
  Iowa who?
Iowa lotta money.

➤ ➤ ➤ ➤ ➤ ➤

Knock-knock.
  Who's there?
Ira.
  Ira who?
Ira sign.

➤ ➤ ➤ ➤ ➤ ➤

Knock-knock.
  Who's there?
Iran.
  Iran who?
Iran all the way!

➤ ➤ ➤ ➤ ➤ ➤

Knock-knock.
  Who's there?
Iraq.
  Iraq who?
Iraq 'n roll.

Knock-knock.
  Who's there?
Irish.
  Irish who?
Irish you a happy St. Patrick's Day.

Knock-knock.
  Who's there?
Isaac.
  Isaac who?
Isaac and tired of these knock-knock jokes.

Knock-knock.
  Who's there?
Isabelle.
  Isabelle who?
Isabelle on a fire engine necessary?

Knock-knock.
  Who's there?
Ismail.
  Ismail who?
Ismail for you.

Knock-knock.
  Who's there?
Israel.
  Israel who?
Israel great to see you again.

  Knock-knock.
    Who's there?
  Huron.
    Huron who?
  Huron my mind.

Knock-knock.
  Who's there?
Ivan.
  Ivan who?
"Ivan working on the railroad."

Knock-knock.
  Who's there?
Ivana.
  Ivana who?
Ivana million dollars.

Knock-knock.
  Who's there?
Roland.
  Roland who?
Roland in dough.

Knock-knock.
  Who's there?
Ivy League.
  Ivy League who?
Ivy League in you.

◆　🏴　➡　🏴　⬇　◤

Knock-knock.
  Who's there?
I wish.
  I wish who?
I wish setter.

◆　🏴　➡　🏴　⬇　◤

Knock-knock.
  Who's there?
Izzy.
  Izzy who?
Izzy the one for me?

◆　🏴　➡　🏴　⬇　◤

Knock-knock.
  Who's there?
Jamaica.
  Jamaica who?
Jamaica me very happy?

❖ ❖ ❖ ❖ ❖ ❖

Knock-knock.
Who's there?
Jane Fonda.
Jane Fonda who?
"Jane Fonda million-dollar baby in a five-and-ten-cent store."

Knock-knock.
Who's there?
Jerome Lee.
Jerome Lee who?
Jerome Lee young once.

Knock-knock.
Who's there?
Jest.
Jest who?
Jest one of those things.

Knock-knock.
Who's there?
Jester.
Jester who?
"Jester spoonful of sugar helps the
medicine go down."

❖   ✦   ➪   ✤   ✦   ✦

Knock-knock.
Who's there?
Jewel.
Jewel who?
Jewel never know what I was going to say.

❖   ✦   ➪   ✤   ✦   ✦

Knock-knock.
Who's there?
Jimmy.
Jimmy who?
"Jimmy your tired, your poor, your
huddled masses yearning to breathe free."

❖   ✦   ➪   ✤   ✦   ✦

Knock-knock.
  Who's there?
Josh.
  Josh who?
Josh me.

Knock-knock.
   Who's there?
Saul.
   Saul who?
"Just me, that's Saul."

Knock-knock.
   Who's there?
Juan.
   Juan who?
Juan of your friends.

Knock-knock.
　Who's there?
Juicy.
　Juicy who?
Juicy any four-leaf clovers?

Knock-knock.
　Who's there?
Juliet.
　Juliet who?
Juliet five hamburgers.

Knock-knock.
　Who's there?
July.
　July who?
July to me?

Knock-knock.
Who's there?
Juneau.
Juneau who?
Juneau any good knock-knock jokes?

Knock-knock.
Who's there?
Soda.
Soda who?
Soda you like knock-knock jokes?

Knock-knock.
Who's there?
Juno.
Juno who?
Juno it's cold out here!

Knock-knock.
   Who's there?
Just Ghost.
   Just Ghost who?
Just Ghost to show you.

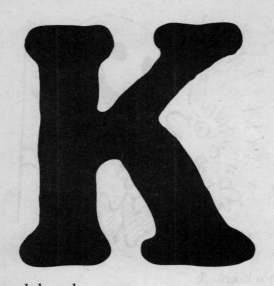

Knock-knock.
  Who's there?
Kalamazoo.
  Kalamazoo who?
Kalamazoo to see the lion's cage.

Knock-knock.
  Who's there?
Kansas.
  Kansas who?
Kansas really be happening to me?

Knock-knock.
  Who's there?
Kareem.
  Kareem who?
Kareem of wheat.

Knock-knock.
  Who's there?
Ken.
  Ken who?
Ken you open the door?

Knock-knock.
  Who's there?
Kent.
  Kent who?
Kent have your cake and eat it too.

✦　✦　➡　✦　⬇　✦

Knock-knock.
  Who's there?
Kenya.
  Kenya who?
Kenya keep a secret?

✦　✦　➡　✦　⬇　✦

Knock-knock.
  Who's there?
Ketchup.
  Ketchup who?
Ketchup with you later.

✦　✦　➡　✦　⬇　✦

Knock-knock.
  Who's there?
Kismet.
  Kismet who?
"Kismet once and kismet twice and kismet
once again."

❧ ❧ ❧ ❧ ❧ ❧

Knock-knock.
  Who's there?
Kissinger.
  Kissinger who?
"I wonder who's Kissinger her now."

♠   ♯   ➡   ♟   ⬇   ♞

Knock-knock.
  Who's there?
Kitchen, kitchen.
  Kitchen, kitchen who?
Don't do that, I'm ticklish.

♠   ♯   ➡   ♟   ⬇   ♞

Knock-knock.
  Who's there?
Kleenex.
  Kleenex who?
Kleenex are prettier than dirty ones.

♠   ♯   ➡   ♟   ⬇   ♞

Knock-knock.
  Who's there?
Kuwait.
  Kuwait who?
Kuwait a minute; I'm on the phone!

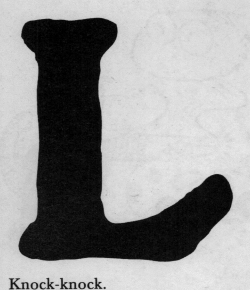

Knock-knock.
  Who's there?
Leggo.
  Leggo who?
Leggo the door, so I can come in.

Knock-knock.
Who's there?
Leif.
Leif who?
Leif me alone.

Knock-knock.
Who's there?
Lena.
Lena who?
Lena tower of Pisa.

Knock-knock.
Who's there?
Lennie.
Lennie who?
Lennie in and you'll see.

Knock-knock.
  Who's there?
Leon.
  Leon who?
Leon me when you're feeling faint.

Knock-knock.
  Who's there?
Les.
  Les who?
Les get out of here.

Knock-knock.
  Who's there?
Lettie.
  Lettie who?
Lettie cat out of the bag.

Knock-knock.
  Who's there?
Lettuce.
  Lettuce who?
Lettuce begin.

Knock-knock.
  Who's there?
Lewis.
  Lewis who?
Lewis lips sink ships.

Knock-knock.
  Who's there?
License.
  License who?
I haven't told a license I was ten.

Knock-knock.
  Who's there?
Lima Bean.
  Lima Bean who?
Lima Bean too busy to call.

✦　✦　✦　✦　✦　✦

Knock-knock.
  Who's there?
Lion.
  Lion who?
Lion like that isn't right.

✦　✦　✦　✦　✦　✦

Knock-knock.
  Who's there?
Lionel.
  Lionel who?
Lionel roar if you don't feed it.

✦　✦　✦　✦　✦　✦

Knock-knock.
   Who's there?
Lisa.
   Lisa who?
Lisa car before you travel.

Knock-knock.
  Who's there?
Liver.
  Liver who?
"Liver stay 'way from my door."

Knock-knock.
  Who's there?
Llama.
  Llama who?
"Llama Yankee Doodle Dandy."

Knock-knock.
  Who's there?
Load.
  Load who?
Load down dirty shame.

Knock-knock.
  Who's there?
Locker.
  Locker who?
Locker up and throw away the key.

❖　　🔳　　➡　　🔳　　⬇　　🔳

Knock-knock.
  Who's there?
Lois.
  Lois who?
Lois the opposite of high.

❖　　🔳　　➡　　🔳　　⬇　　🔳

Knock-knock.
  Who's there?
Lo Mein.
  Lo Mein who?
Lo Mein on the totem pole.

❖　　🔳　　➡　　🔳　　⬇　　🔳

Knock-knock.
  Who's there?
Lorne.
  Lorne who?
Lorne order.

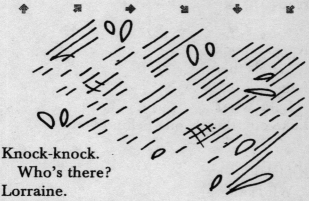

Knock-knock.
  Who's there?
Lorraine.
  Lorraine who?
"Lorraine in Spain stays mainly in the plain."

Knock-knock.
  Who's there?
Louisville.
  Louisville who?
Louisville come when he's good and
ready.

Knock-knock.
  Who's there?
Luke.
  Luke who?
Luke out, there's one behind you.

Knock-knock.
  Who's there?
Lyle.
  Lyle who?
"Lyle string along with you."

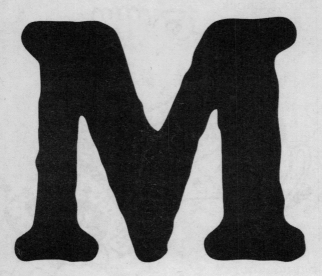

Knock-knock.
  Who's there?
Macho.
  Macho who?
"Macho-do about nothing."

Knock-knock.
  Who's there?
Madison.
  Madison who?
Madison will cure me of my cough.

Knock-knock.
  Who's there?
Maiden.
  Maiden who?
Maiden Japan.

Knock-knock.
  Who's there?
Maiden.
  Maiden who?
Maiden the shade.

Knock-knock.
　Who's there?
Major.
　Major who?
"Major days be merry and bright..."

❀　　❀　　❀　　❀　　❀　　❀

Knock-knock.
　Who's there?
Mangoes.
　Mangoes who?
Mangoes crazy.

❀　　❀　　❀　　❀　　❀　　❀

Knock-knock.
　Who's there?
Manna.
　Manna who?
Manna mouse, which are you?

❀　　❀　　❀　　❀　　❀　　❀

Knock-knock.
  Who's there?
Mary Hannah.
  Mary Hannah who?
Mary Hannah little lamb.

Knock-knock.
  Who's there?
Mary Lee.
  Mary Lee who?
"Mary Lee we roll along."

⬆   ⬈   ➡   ⬊   ⬇   ⬋

Knock-knock.
  Who's there?
Matilda.
  Matilda who?
"Matilda end of time."

⬆   ⬈   ➡   ⬊   ⬇   ⬋

Knock-knock.
  Who's there?
Maud.
  Maud who?
Maud as a hatter.

⬆   ⬈   ➡   ⬊   ⬇   ⬋

Knock-knock.
  Who's there?
Maura.
  Maura who?
Maura see you, Maura like you.

Knock-knock.
  Who's there?
Maura.
  Maura who?
Maura less.

Knock-knock.
Who's there?
Maya.
Maya who?
Maya never darken my door again.

Knock-knock.
  Who's there?
Mega.
  Mega who?
Mega the bed, I wanna go to sleep.

Knock-knock.
  Who's there?
Megan.
  Megan who?
Megan end to these knock-knocks.

Knock-knock.
  Who's there?
Melrose.
  Melrose who?
Melrose when I put a tack on his seat.

Knock-knock.
  Who's there?
Mike.
  Mike who?
Mike makes right.

Knock-knock.
  Who's there?
Mike.
  Mike who?
Mike kind of town, Chicago is.

Knock-knock.
  Who's there?
Miners.
  Miners who?
Miners yours, and yours are mine.

Knock-knock.
  Who's there?
Minnie.
  Minnie who?
Minnie are called but few are chosen.

Knock-knock.
  Who's there?
Mister.
  Mister who?
Mister by that much.

Knock-knock.
  Who's there?
Moose.
  Moose who?
Moose be magic.

✦　✦　➡　✦　✦　✦

Knock-knock.
  Who's there?
Moppet.
  Moppet who?
Moppet up before it gets sticky.

♠ ⚐ ➡ ⚑ ⬇ ⚐

Knock-knock.
  Who's there?
Mrs.
  Mrs. who?
Mrs. as good as a mile.

♠ ⚐ ➡ ⚑ ⬇ ⚐

Knock-knock.
  Who's there?
Mummy.
  Mummy who?
Mummy burns a hole in my pocket.

Knock-knock.
  Who's there?
Hugh.
  Hugh who?
Hugh can't take it with you.

⬆ ⬈ ➡ ⬊ ⬇ ⬋

Knock-knock.
  Who's there?
Murray.
  Murray who?
Murray Christmas.

⬆ ⬈ ➡ ⬊ ⬇ ⬋

Knock-knock.
  Who's there?
Musket.
  Musket who?
Musket my coat. I'm freezing.

⬆ ⬈ ➡ ⬊ ⬇ ⬋

Knock-knock.
  Who's there?
Mustache.
  Mustache who?
Mustache, I'm in a hurry.

Knock-knock.
  Who's there?
Myth.
  Myth who?
Myth me when I was gone?

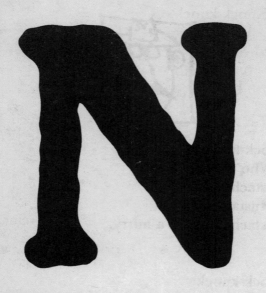

Knock-knock.
   Who's there?
Nero.
   Nero who?
"Nero my God to thee."

Knock-knock.
  Who's there?
Owen.
  Owen who?
"Owen the Saints go marching in."

  ⬆   ↗   ➡   ↘   ⬇   ↙

Knock-knock.
  Who's there?
Never-Never Land.
  Never-Never Land who?
Never-Never Land money to a stranger.

  ⬆   ↗   ➡   ↘   ⬇   ↙

Knock-knock.
  Who's there?
Newton.
  Newton who?
Newton doing.

  ⬆   ↗   ➡   ↘   ⬇   ↙

Knock-knock.
 Who's there?
Niacin.
 Niacin who?
Niacin easy does it every time.

Knock-knock.
  Who's there?
Noah.
  Noah who?
Noah good place to eat around here?

✦   ✖   ➡   ✖   ⬇   ✖

Knock-knock.
  Who's there?
Noah.
  Noah who?
Noah body here but us chickens.

✦   ✖   ➡   ✖   ⬇   ✖

Knock-knock.
  Who's there?
Nona.
  Nona who?
Nona your business.

✦   ✖   ➡   ✖   ⬇   ✖

Knock-knock.
  Who's there?
Norman.
  Norman who?
Norman is an island.

Knock-knock.
  Who's there?
Norway.
  Norway who?
Norway are you going to open the door.

Knock-knock.
  Who's there?
Noun.
  Noun who?
Noun then.

Knock-knock.
  Who's there?
Nuisance.
  Nuisance who?
What's nuisance yesterday?

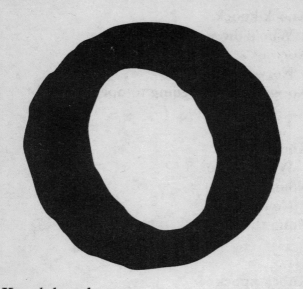

Knock-knock.
  Who's there?
Odessa.
  Odessa who?
Odessa awful thing to say.

Knock-knock.

Who's there?

Odor.

Odor who?

"Odor sun shines bright on pretty redwing."

Knock-knock.

Who's there?

Odyssey.

Odyssey who?

Odyssey the movie I saw last night.

Knock-knock.

Who's there?

Ohio.

Ohio who?

Ohio miss you tonight.

Knock-knock.
　Who's there?
Oil.
　Oil who?
Oil in the family.

Knock-knock.
  Who's there?
Oily.
  Oily who?
Oily to bed, oily to rise.

Knock-knock.
  Who's there?
Oink, Oink.
  Oink, Oink who?
Are you a pig or an owl?

Knock-knock.
  Who's there?
Olga.
  Olga who?
Olga round to the back door.

Knock-knock.
  Who's there?
Olive.
  Olive who?
Olive on the other side of town.

Knock-knock.
  Who's there?
Oliver.
  Oliver who?
Oliver the world people are telling knock-knock jokes.

Knock-knock.
  Who's there?
Oman.
  Oman who?
Oman! Did you see that?

Knock-knock.
  Who's there?
Omelet.
  Omelet who?
Omelet smarter than I look.

Knock-knock.
  Who's there?
Omen.
  Omen who?
"Omen river, that Omen river."

✦ ✦ ✦ ✦ ✦ ✦

Knock-knock.
  Who's there?
Ona Clare.
  Ona Clare who?
"Ona Clare day you can see forever."

✦ ✦ ✦ ✦ ✦ ✦

Knock-knock.
  Who's there?
Ooze.
  Ooze who?
"Ooze afraid of the big, bad wolf?"

✦ ✦ ✦ ✦ ✦ ✦

Knock-knock.
  Who's there?
Orange.
  Orange who?
Orange you going out tonight?

Knock-knock.

Who's there?

Order.

Order who?

"Order land of the free and the home of the brave."

Knock-knock.
  Who's there?
Osborne.
  Osborne who?
Osborne in the U.S.A.

  Knock-knock.
    Who's there?
  Emma.
    Emma who?
  "Emma Yankee Doodle Dandy."

✦   ✺   ➧   ✺   ✦   ✺

Knock-knock.
  Who's there?
Oscar.
  Oscar who?
Oscar if she has a sister.

✦   ✺   ➧   ✺   ✦   ✺

Knock-knock.
  Who's there?
Ostrich.
  Ostrich who?
Ostrich my pants so far, they ripped.

Knock-knock.
  Who's there?
Otis.
  Otis who?
Otis is a great day for a picnic.

Knock-knock.
  Who's there?
Ida.
  Ida who?
Ida wanna go to school.

Knock-knock.

Who's there?

Otto.

Otto who?

Otto be more alert when strangers are at the door.

Knock-knock.
   Who's there?
Owen.
   Owen who?
Owen my way?

Knock-knock.
   Who's there?
Owl.
   Owl who?
Owl be seeing you.

Knock-knock.
  Who's there?
Garter.
  Garter who?
Garter go.

Knock-knock.
  Who's there?
Owl go.
  Owl go who?
Yes, I know they do.

Knock-knock.
  Who's there?
Ozzie.
  Ozzie who?
Ozzie you around.

Knock-knock.
  Who's there?
Pasta.
  Pasta who?
Pasta salt, please.

Knock-knock.
  Who's there?
Pear.
  Pear who?
Pear-haps I'll see you later.

Knock-knock.
  Who's there?
Pear.
  Pear who?
Pear of shoes.

  Knock-knock.
    Who's there?
  Shoes.
    Shoes who?
  Shoes me. Did I step on your foot?

Knock-knock.
  Who's there?
Pecan.
  Pecan who?
Pecan choose.

⬆ ⬈ ➡ ⬊ ⬇ ⬋

Knock-knock.
  Who's there?
Pencil.
  Pencil who?
Pencil fall down if you don't wear a belt.

⬆ ⬈ ➡ ⬊ ⬇ ⬋

Knock-knock.
  Who's there?
Peony.
  Peony who?
Peony saved is a peony earned.

⬆ ⬈ ➡ ⬊ ⬇ ⬋

Knock-knock.
  Who's there?
Pepper.
  Pepper who?
Pepper up. She looks tired.

Knock-knock.
  Who's there?
Pest.
  Pest who?
Pest things in life are free.

Knock-knock.
  Who's there?
Pharaoh.
  Pharaoh who?
Pharaoh way places.

Knock-knock.
  Who's there?
Phillip.
  Phillip who?
Phillip the tank, we've got a long way to go.

Knock-knock.
　Who's there?
Phyllis.
　Phyllis who?
Phyllis form out and return it to me.

Knock-knock.
　Who's there?
Pig.
　Pig who?
Pig up your feet when you walk.

Knock-knock.
  Who's there?
Piranha.
  Piranha who?
"Piranha old-gray bonnet."

✦   ✦   ✦   ✦   ✦   ✦

Knock-knock.
  Who's there?
Pizza.
  Pizza who?
Pizza that apple pie would be nice.

🐦 🪁 ➡️ 🐦 ⬇️ 🐦

Knock-knock.
  Who's there?
Play Dough.
  Play Dough who?
Play Dough was a famous Greek
philosopher.

  Knock-knock.
    Who's there?
  Saul.
    Saul who?
  Saul Greek to me.

🐦 🪁 ➡️ 🐦 ⬇️ 🐦

Knock-knock.
  Who's there?
Police.
  Police who?
Police answer the door.

Knock-knock.
  Who's there?
Irish Stew.
  Irish Stew who?
Irish Stew in the name of the law.

Knock-knock
   Who's there?
Police.
   Police who?
"Police release me, let me go."

Knock-knock.
   Who's there?
Police.
   Police who?
Police don't talk about me when I'm gone.

Knock-knock.
   Who's there?
Pollyanna.
   Pollyanna who?
Pollyanna bad kid when you get to know her.

Knock-knock.
  Who's there?
Polyp.
  Polyp who?
Polyp your socks, they're falling down.

Knock-knock.
  Who's there?
Possum.
  Possum who?
Possum ketchup on my burger.

Knock-knock.
  Who's there?
Pressure.
  Pressure who?
Pressure shirt.

Knock-knock.
   Who's there?
Psalm.
   Psalm who?
"Psalm where over the rainbow."

Knock-knock.
  Who's there?
Quiche.
  Quiche who?
Quiche me, you fool.

Knock-knock.
  Who's there?
Lennie.
  Lennie who?
Lennie kiss you.

Knock-knock.
  Who's there?
Quebec.
  Quebec who?
Quebec to square one.

Knock-knock.
  Who's there?
Queen.
  Queen who?
Queen up your room.

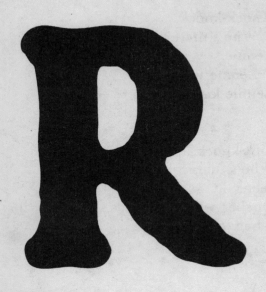

Knock-knock.
    Who's there?
Racine.
    Racine who?
"Racine with the moon."

Knock-knock.
  Who's there?
Wendy.
  Wendy who?
"Wendy moon comes over the mountain."

Knock-knock.
  Who's there?
Raisin.
  Raisin who?
Raisin a racket with all that noise.

Knock-knock.
  Who's there?
Rapture.
  Rapture who?
Rapture presents with a large bow.

Knock-knock.
  Who's there?
Raul.
  Raul who?
Raul out the barrel.

↑   ↘   →   ↘   ↓   ↙

Knock-knock.
  Who's there?
Ray.
  Ray who?
"Ray who," said the mixed-up cheerleader.

↑   ↘   →   ↘   ↓   ↙

Knock-knock.
  Who's there?
Razor.
  Razor who?
Razor curtain and let the sun in.

Knock-knock.
  Who's there?
Delight.
  Delight who?
Delight is hurting my eyes.

Knock-knock.
  Who's there?
Repeat.
  Repeat who?
Who, who, who, who.

⬆ ⬈ ➡ ⬊ ⬇ ⬃

Knock-knock.
  Who's there?
Rhino.
  Rhino who?
"Rhino a dark, secluded place."

⬆ ⬈ ➡ ⬊ ⬇ ⬃

Knock-knock.
  Who's there?
Rhoda.
  Rhoda who?
Rhoda horse last week.

⬆ ⬈ ➡ ⬊ ⬇ ⬃

Knock-knock.
  Who's there?
Rhonda.
  Rhonda who?
Rhonda first base when you hit the ball.

Knock-knock.
  Who's there?
Rice.
  Rice who?
Rice and shine.

Knock-knock.
  Who's there?
Roach.
  Roach who?
Roach you a letter but you didn't write
back.

Knock-knock.
  Who's there?
Robinson Crusoe.
  Robinson Crusoe who?
Robinson Crusoe big he had to buy larger jeans.

Knock-knock.
  Who's there?
Rocco.
  Rocco who?
"Rocco round the clock."

Knock-knock.
  Who's there?
Roland.
  Roland who?
Roland stone gathers no moss.

Knock-knock.
  Who's there?
Ron D.
  Ron D. who?
Ron D. vu.

Knock-knock.
  Who's there?
Rona.
  Rona who?
Rona boat is hard work.

Knock-knock.
  Who's there?
Root.
  Root who?
"Root, root, root for the home team."

Knock-knock.
  Who's there?
Rough.
  Rough who?
"Rough to see the wizard."

Knock-knock.
  Who's there?
Roxanne.
  Roxanne who?
Roxanne pebbles are in my shoes.

Knock-knock.
  Who's there?
Russell.
  Russell who?
Russell me up something to eat.

Knock-knock.
  Who's there?
Jamaica.
  Jamaica who?
Jamaica dinner? I'm starving.

✦ ✦ ➧ ✦ ⬇ ✦

Knock-knock.
  Who's there?
Russia.
  Russia who?
Russia large pizza to this address.

✦ ✦ ➧ ✦ ⬇ ✦

Knock-knock.
  Who's there?
Ryan.
  Ryan who?
Ryan you return my phone calls?

✦ ✦ ➧ ✦ ⬇ ✦

Knock-knock.
    Who's there?
Saber.
    Saber who?
Saber—she's drowning.

Knock-knock.
    Who's there?
Eiffel.
    Eiffel who?
Eiffel into the lake.

♠   ♜   ➡   ♞   ⬇   ♞

Knock-knock.
  Who's there?
Sahara.
  Sahara who?
Sahara you today?

Knock-knock.
    Who's there?
Freddy.
    Freddy who?
Freddy, willing, and able.

♠   ♜   ➡   ♞   ⬇   ♞

Knock-knock.
   Who's there?
Saint.
   Saint who?
"Saint necessarily so."

✦   ⬈   ➡   ⬊   ⬇   ⬈

Knock-knock.
   Who's there?
Sam.
   Sam who?
Sam person who just knocked, silly!

✦   ⬈   ➡   ⬊   ⬇   ⬈

Knock-knock.
   Who's there?
Samantha.
   Samantha who?
Samantha fix the T.V.

✦   ⬈   ➡   ⬊   ⬇   ⬈

Knock-knock.
  Who's there?
Sanitize.
  Sanitize who?
Sanitize his reindeer to a sled.

Knock-knock.
   Who's there?
Sanity.
   Sanity who?
Sanity Claus.

Knock-knock.
   Who's there?
Ali.
   Ali who?
"Ali want for Christmas are my two
front teeth."

Knock-knock.
  Who's there?
Sarah.
  Sarah who?
Sarah extra key? I lost mine.

Knock-knock.
  Who's there?
Sarong.
  Sarong who?
Sarong number; dial again.

  Knock-knock.
    Who's there?
  Duet.
    Duet who?
  Duet right.

Knock-knock.

Who's there?

Sasha.

Sasha who?

Sasha fuss, just because I knocked on your door.

Knock-knock.

Who's there?

Doris.

Doris who?

Doris closed so I knocked.

🔼   🔁   ➡   🔀   🔽   ↘

Knock-knock.

Who's there?

Saul.

Saul who?

Saul over town that you won't open the door.

🔼   🔁   ➡   🔀   🔽   ↘

Knock-knock.
  Who's there?
Sawyer.
  Sawyer who?
Sawyer picture in the paper.

Knock-knock.
  Who's there?
Scold.
  Scold who?
Scold enough to know better.

Knock-knock.
  Who's there?
Scott.
  Scott who?
"Scott the whole world in his hands."

Scratch, scratch.
  Who's there?
I'm too weak to knock.

Knock-knock.
  Who's there?
Séance.
  Séance who?
Séance fiction.

Knock-knock.
  Who's there?
Senior.
  Senior who?
Senior ad in the paper.

Knock-knock.
  Who's there?
Seymour.
  Seymour who?
Seymour monkeys at the zoo.

✦   ✦   ✦   ✦   ✦   ✦

Knock-knock.
Who's there?
Sheik.
Sheik who?
Sheik and you shall find.

Knock-knock.
Who's there?
Sheila.
Sheila who?
"Sheila be coming round the mountain
when she comes."

Knock-knock.
Who's there?
Shelby.
Shelby who?
Shelby take a walk?

Knock-knock.
Who's there?
Sherwood.
Sherwood who?
Sherwood like a cold drink.

Knock-knock.
Who's there?
Shirley.
Shirley who?
Shirley you must be joking.

Knock-knock.
Who's there?
Shoe.
Shoe who?
"Shoe me the way to go home."

Knock-knock.
Who's there?
Shore.
Shore who?
Shore would like it if you bought me a burger.

Knock-knock.
Who's there?
Sid.
Sid who?
Sid down and be quiet.

Knock-knock.
  Who's there?
Simms.
  Simms who?
"Simms like old times."

✦   🎜   ➡   🎜   ⬇   🎜

Knock-knock.
  Who's there?
Simon.
  Simon who?
"Simon love with a wonderful guy."

✦   🎜   ➡   🎜   ⬇   🎜

Knock-knock.
  Who's there?
Singapore.
  Singapore who?
You Singapore and I don't want to listen.

✦   🎜   ➡   🎜   ⬇   🎜

Knock-knock.
　Who's there?
Sir.
　Sir who?
Sir-prize!

➤　➤　➤　➤　➤　➤

Knock-knock.
Who's there?
Skit.
Skit who?
Skit this show on the road.

Knock-knock.
Who's there?
Snake.
Snake who?
"Snake me out to the ball game."

Knock-knock.
   Who's there?
Hannibal.
   Hannibal who?
Hannibal game will last nine innings.

♠ ♆ ➡ ♆ ⬇ ♆

Knock-knock.
   Who's there?
Sneer.
   Sneer who?
Sneer and yet so far.

♠ ♆ ➡ ♆ ⬇ ♆

Knock-knock.
   Who's there?
Soda.
   Soda who?
Soda you want me to write you a letter?

♠ ♆ ➡ ♆ ⬇ ♆

Knock-knock.
  Who's there?
Sol.
  Sol who?
Sol there is, there ain't no more.

Knock-knock.
  Who's there?
Sole.
  Sole who?
Sole new ball game.

Knock-knock.
  Who's there?
Solo.
  Solo who?
Solo, I can't reach the doorbell.

Knock-knock.
　Who's there?
Sony.
　Sony who?
Sony me knocking.

Knock-knock.
 Who's there?
Spider.
 Spider who?
Spider what everyone says, I like you.

⬆ ⬈ ➡ ⬊ ⬇ ⬋

Knock-knock.
 Who's there?
Spin.
 Spin who?
Spin a long time since we met.

⬆ ⬈ ➡ ⬊ ⬇ ⬋

Knock-knock.
   Who's there?
Stefan.
   Stefan who?
"Stefan out with my baby."

♠   ♜   ♦   ♞   ♥   ♝

Knock-knock.
   Who's there?
Stella.
   Stella who?
Stella waters run deep.

♠   ♜   ♦   ♞   ♥   ♝

Knock-knock.
   Who's there?
Stu.
   Stu who?
Stu close for comfort.

♠   ♜   ♦   ♞   ♥   ♝

Knock-knock.
Who's there?
Succumb.
Succumb who?
Succumb up and see me sometime.

♦ ♦ ♦ ♦ ♦ ♦

Knock-knock.
Who's there?
Sue.
Sue who?
Don't ask me, I'm not a lawyer.

♦ ♦ ♦ ♦ ♦ ♦

Knock-knock.
Who's there?
Suede.
Suede who?
"Suede down south in Dixie."

♦ ♦ ♦ ♦ ♦ ♦

Knock-knock.
  Who's there?
Summer.
  Summer who?
Summer chosen, summer not.

✦　✦　➡　↘　⬇　↙

Knock-knock.
  Who's there?
Summer.
  Summer who?
Summer my best friends go to that school.

✦　✦　➡　↘　⬇　↙

Knock-knock.
  Who's there?
Summons.
  Summons who?
"Summons to watch over me."

Knock-knock.
  Who's there?
Sup.
  Sup who?
Sup to me.

Knock-knock.
Who's there?
Surly.
Surly who?
Surly in the morning; go back to bed.

Knock-knock.
Who's there?
Suture.
Suture who?
Suture self.

Knock-knock.
Who's there?
Swarm.
Swarm who?
Swarm in the summer and scold in the winter.

Knock-knock.
  Who's there?
Swatter.
  Swatter who?
"Swatter difference a day makes."

Knock-knock.
  Who's there?
Sweden.
  Sweden who?
Sweden my cocoa.

Knock-knock.
  Who's there?
Sweden.
  Sweden who?
Sweden sour pork.

Knock-knock.
 Who's there?
Switch.
 Switch who?
Switch craft.

Knock-knock.
  Who's there?
Taint.
  Taint who?
Taint over till it's over.

Knock-knock.
  Who's there?
Taiwan.
  Taiwan who?
Taiwan to be happy.

Knock-knock.
  Who's there?
Tally.
  Tally who?
What are you, a fox hunter?

Knock-knock.
  Who's there?
Tamara.
  Tamara who?
Tamara is another day.

Knock-knock.
  Who's there?
Tammany.
  Tammany who?
Tammany cooks spoil the broth.

Knock-knock.
  Who's there?
Tanks.
  Tanks who?
"Tanks for the memories."

Knock-knock.
  Who's there?
Targets.
  Targets who?
Targets on my shoes when I walk on new asphalt.

Knock-knock.
  Who's there?
Tennis.
  Tennis who?
Tennis larger than nine.

Knock-knock.
  Who's there?
Terrain.
  Terrain who?
"Terrain in Spain stays mainly in the plain."

♠ ♩ ➡ ♞ ♦ ♜

Knock-knock.
  Who's there?
Terrify Tish.
  Terrify Tish who?
Well, maybe just a little one on the cheek.

♠ ♩ ➡ ♞ ♦ ♜

Knock-knock.
  Who's there?
Texas.
  Texas who?
Texas a long time to get together.

♠ ♩ ➡ ♞ ♦ ♜

Knock-knock.
  Who's there?
Thames.
  Thames who?
Thames da breaks.

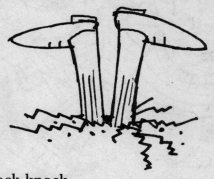

Knock-knock.
  Who's there?
Juneau.
  Juneau who?
Juneau something I don't know?

Knock-knock.
　Who's there?
Thatcher.
　Thatcher who?
"Thatcher falling star and put it in your pocket."

Knock-knock.
　Who's there?
The ants are.
　The ants are who?
"The ants are, my friend, is blowing in the wind."

Knock-knock.
　Who's there?
Theresa.
　Theresa who?
Theresa pretty around here.

Knock-knock.
　Who's there?
Thermos.
　Thermos who?
Thermos be a better way.

Knock-knock.
  Who's there?
Thesis.
  Thesis who?
Thesis a stickup.

Knock-knock.
  Who's there?
Jimmy.
  Jimmy who?
Jimmy all your money!

Knock-knock.
  Who's there?
Think?
  Think who?
Think or thwim.

Knock-knock.
  Who's there?
Thistle.
  Thistle who?
"Thistle man came rolling home."

Knock-knock.
  Who's there?
Thomas.
  Thomas who?
Thomas of the essence.

Knock-knock.
    Who's there?
Thor.
    Thor who?
Thor from head to toe.

Knock-knock.
   Who's there?
Thumb.
   Thumb who?
"Thumb enchanted evening."

   Knock-knock.
      Who's there?
Dishes.
   Dishes who?
"Dishes a lovely way to spend an
evening."

✦   ⤢   ➡   ✦   ⬇   ✦

Knock-knock.
   Who's there?
Tibet.
   Tibet who?
You want Tibet?

✦   ⤢   ➡   ✦   ⬇   ✦

Knock-knock.
   Who's there?
Tijuana.
   Tijuana who?
Tijuana ride my bike?

♠   ♞   ➡   ♜   ⬇   ♝

Knock-knock.
   Who's there?
Tim.
   Tim who?
Tim-burr!

♠   ♞   ➡   ♜   ⬇   ♝

Knock-knock.
   Who's there?
Tire.
   Tire who?
"Tire yellow ribbon round the old oak
tree."

♠   ♞   ➡   ♜   ⬇   ♝

Knock-knock.
  Who's there?
Titan.
  Titan who?
Titan your seat belt.

Knock-knock.
  Who's there?
Toboggan.
  Toboggan who?
Don't try Toboggan
with me.

Knock-knock.

Who's there?

Tom Sawyer.

Tom Sawyer who?

Tom Sawyer looking at his homework.

Knock-knock.
  Who's there?
Trees.
  Trees who?
Trees a crowd.

Knock-knock.
  Who's there?
Trigger.
  Trigger who?
Trigger treat.

Knock-knock.
  Who's there?
Trio.
  Trio who?
Trio clock in the morning.

Knock-knock.
  Who's there?
Stella.
  Stella who?
Stella the night.

✦ 🖉 ➡ ◀ ⬇ ◣

Knock-knock.
  Who's there?
Tulsa.
  Tulsa who?
Tulsa story, please.

✦ 🖉 ➡ ◀ ⬇ ◣

Knock-knock.
  Who's there?
Turner.
  Turner who?
Turner round, I can't stand your face.

✦ 🖉 ➡ ◀ ⬇ ◣

Knock-knock.
  Who's there?
Turnip.
  Turnip who?
Turnip the radio, I can't hear the words.

Knock-knock.
  Who's there?
Twain.
  Twain who?
Twain your dog to do tricks.

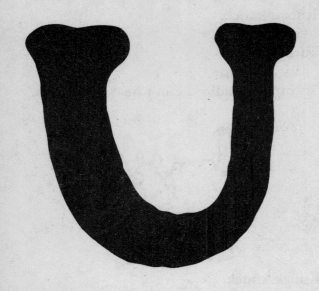

Knock-knock.
  Who's there?
Uganda.
  Uganda who?
Uganda come to my party?

Knock-knock.
  Who's there?
Oscar.
  Oscar who?
Oscar if she wants to come to my party.

✦　✦　➡　✦　⬇　✦

Knock-knock.
  Who's there?
Unaware.
  Unaware who?
Unaware is what you put on first in the morning.

✦　✦　➡　✦　⬇　✦

Knock-knock.
  Who's there?
Uneeda.
  Uneeda who?
Uneeda haircut.

Knock-knock.
   Who's there?
Harris.
   Harris who?
Harris nice to have on the top of your
head.

♠   ♯   ➡   ♫   ♪   ✦

Knock-knock.
  Who's there?
Unit.
  Unit who?
Unit a lovely sweater.

✦ 🡕 ➡ 🡖 🡓 🡖

Knock-knock.
  Who's there?
Upton.
  Upton who?
Upton girl looking for a downtown man.

✦ 🡕 ➡ 🡖 🡓 🡖

Knock-knock.
  Who's there?
Utica.
  Utica who?
Utica second piece of cake?

✦ 🡕 ➡ 🡖 🡓 🡖

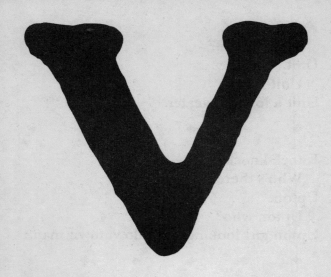

Knock-knock.
   Who's there?
Valencia.
   Valencia who?
Valencia a dollar, will you pay me back?

Knock-knock.
  Who's there?
Van Nuys.
  Van Nuys who?
"Van Nuys was seventeen, it was a very good year."

Knock-knock.
  Who's there?
Vassar.
  Vassar who?
Vassar matter with you?

Knock-knock.
  Who's there?
Vaudeville.
  Vaudeville who?
Vaudeville I ever do without you?

Knock-knock.
  Who's there?
Water.
  Water who?
Water friends for?

♠   ⚑   ➡   ♘   ⬇   ♞

Knock-knock.
  Who's there?
Veal.
  Veal who?
Veal see about that, von't ve?

♠   ⚑   ➡   ♘   ⬇   ♞

Knock-knock.
  Who's there?
Vendor.
  Vendor who?
"Vendor red, red robin comes bob, bob,
bobbin' along."

♠   ⚑   ➡   ♘   ⬇   ♞

Knock-knock.
　Who's there?
Venice.
　Venice who?
Venice lunch?

Knock-knock.
  Who's there?
Wilma.
  Wilma who?
Wilma lunch be ready soon?

❖   ⚑   ➡   ⚑   ⬇   ⬉

Knock-knock.
  Who's there?
Venue.
  Venue who?
"Venue old wedding ring was new."

❖   ⚑   ➡   ⚑   ⬇   ⬉

Knock-knock.
  Who's there?
Vera.
  Vera who?
Vera interesting.

❖   ⚑   ➡   ⚑   ⬇   ⬉

Knock-knock.
Who's there?
Vera.
Vera who?
Vera hat. It's cold outside.

Knock-knock.
Who's there?
Verdi.
Verdi who?
"Verdi boys are."

Knock-knock.
  Who's there?
Verdi.
  Verdi who?
Verdi you get the best pizza in town?

  Knock-knock.
    Who's there?
  Gopher.
    Gopher who?
  Gopher pizza, I'm hungry.

⬆ ⬈ ➡ ⬊ ⬇ ⬋

Knock-knock.
  Who's there?
Victor.
  Victor who?
Victor his pants on the fence.

⬆ ⬈ ➡ ⬊ ⬇ ⬋

Knock-knock.
　Who's there?
Vince.
　Vince who?
Vince some, lose some.

Knock-knock.
Who's there?
Vine.
Vine who?
Vine and dandy.

Knock-knock.
Who's there?
Viola.
Viola who?
Viola fuss, I'm only five minutes late?

Knock-knock.
  Who's there?
Violet.
  Violet who?
Violet myself make these jokes, I don't
understand.

Knock-knock.
  Who's there?
Violin.
  Violin who?
Violin your neighborhood I thought I'd
say hello.

Knock-knock.
  Who's there?
Viper.
  Viper who?
Viper hands, they're still wet.

Knock-knock.
  Who's there?
Vicious.
  Vicious who?
"Vicious you a Merry Christmas."

◆   ⚑   ➡   ⚑   ⬇   ⚑

Knock-knock.
   Who's there?
Vision.
   Vision who?
Vision you would let me in.

Knock-knock.
   Who's there?
Vonce.
   Vonce who?
Vonce upon a time...

Knock-knock.
   Who's there?
Voodoo.
   Voodoo who?
"Voodoo something to me."

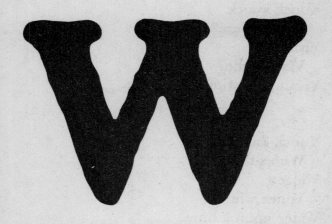

Knock-knock.
  Who's there?
Wa.
  Wa who?
That's right, wahoo! We're having fun
now!

♠ ⚑ ➨ ⚐ ⬇ ⬈

Knock-knock.
  Who's there?
Wade.
  Wade who?
"Wade down upon the Swanee River."

   ⬆   ⬈   ➡   ⬊   ⬇   ⬋

Knock-knock.
  Who's there?
Wanda.
  Wanda who?
Wanda hear another knock-knock?

  Knock-knock.
    Who's there?
  Noah.
    Noah who?
  Noah don't.

   ⬆   ⬈   ➡   ⬊   ⬇   ⬋

Knock-knock.
　Who's there?
Warner.
　Warner who?
"Warner these days, to the moon, Alice."

❦　❦　➡　❦　⬇　❦

Knock-knock.
  Who's there?
Warrant.
  Warrant who?
Warrant you here before?

Knock-knock.
  Who's there?
Warren.
  Warren who?
Warren peace.

Knock-knock.
  Who's there?
Warrior.
  Warrior who?
Warrior been? I've been here for five
minutes.

Knock-knock.
  Who's there?
Warsaw.
  Warsaw who?
Warsaw matter, cat got your tongue?

Knock-knock.
  Who's
there?
Water.
  Water who?
Water difference a day makes.

Knock-knock.
  Who's there?
Watson.
  Watson who?
Watson your mind?

✦ ➤ ➜ ✖ ⬇ ✖

Knock-knock.
  Who's there?
Wayne.
  Wayne who?
"Wayne drops keep falling on my head."

  Knock-knock.
    Who's there?
  Wayne.
    Wayne who?
  "Wayne, Wayne go away, come again
  another day."

✦ ➤ ➜ ✖ ⬇ ✖

Knock-knock.
  Who's there?
Weaken.
  Weaken who?
"Weaken work it out."

Knock-knock.
  Who's there?
Weed.
  Weed who?
Weed better get going.

Knock-knock.
  Who's there?
Weird.
  Weird who?
Weird you get that crazy outfit?

Knock-knock.
  Who's there?
Delaware.
  Delaware who?
Delaware's weird clothes.

Knock-knock.
  Who's there?
Weirdo.
  Weirdo who?
Weirdo we go from here?

Knock-knock.
  Who's there?
Welfare.
  Welfare who?
Welfare crying out loud!

Knock-knock.
　Who's there?
Wendell.
　Wendell who?
Wendell you think it will rain?

Knock-knock.
　Who's there?
Wendy.
　Wendy who?
Wendy cats away, the mouse will play.

Knock-knock.
　Who's there?
Wet.
　Wet who?
Wet me in, it's raining.

Knock-knock.
  Who's there?
Whale.
  Whale who?
Whale it's awfully nice to see you again.

* * * * * *

Knock-knock.
  Who's there?
Wheel.
  Wheel who?
Wheel stop knocking if you open up.

* * * * * *

Knock-knock.
  Who's there?
Whitmore.
  Whitmore who?
Whitmore do you want?

* * * * * *

Knock-knock.
  Who's there?
Whoa.
  Whoa who?
"Whoa, whoa, whoa your boat gently
down the stream."

Knock-knock.
  Who's there?
Wilfred.
  Wilfred who?
Wilfred call me tonight?

Knock-knock.
  Who's there?
Willy.
  Willy who?
Willy or won't he?

Knock-knock.
  Who's there?
Willis.
  Willis who?
Willis be the beginning of a friendship?

  Knock-knock.
    Who's there?
  Kent.
    Kent who?
  Kent we be friends?

Knock-knock.
  Who's there?
Willoughby.
  Willoughby who?
Willoughby no or yes?

Knock-knock.
  Who's there?
Noah.
  Noah who?
Noah yes—which is it?

♠ ♜ ➡ ♞ ⬇ ♟

Knock-knock.
  Who's there?
Wilma.
  Wilma who?
Wilma movie be on TV tonight?

♠ ♜ ➡ ♞ ⬇ ♟

Knock-knock.
  Who's there?
Wilma.
  Wilma who?
Wilma ship ever come in?

♠ ♜ ➡ ♞ ⬇ ♟

Knock-knock.
  Who's there?
Window.
  Window who?
Window we eat?

Knock-knock.
  Who's there?
Winnie.
  Winnie who?
Winnie you going to think up a better
knock-knock joke?

✦ ◪ ➡ ◪ ⬇ ◪

Knock-knock.
  Who's there?
Wise.
  Wise who?
Wise everybody always picking on me?

✦ ◪ ➡ ◪ ⬇ ◪

Knock-knock.
  Who's there?
Wooden shoe.
  Wooden shoe who?
Wooden shoe really like a cold drink?

✦ ◪ ➡ ◪ ⬇ ◪

Knock-knock.
  Who's there?
Wren.
  Wren who?
Wren are you coming over?

Knock-knock.
  Who's there?
X.
  X who?
X me no questions, I'll tell you no lies.

❖ ⚑ ➡ ⚑ ❖ ⚑

Knock-knock.
  Who's there?
Xavier.
  Xavier who?
Xavier money for a rainy day.

  Knock-knock.
    Who's there?
  Thomas.
    Thomas who?
  Thomas money.

  ♠ ↗ ➡ ↘ ↓ ↙

Knock-knock.
  Who's there?
Xylophone.
  Xylophone who?
Xylophone and call me.

  ♠ ↗ ➡ ↘ ↓ ↙

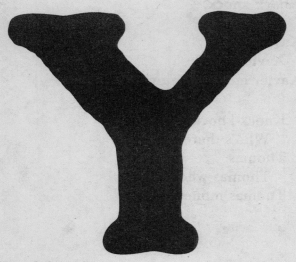

Knock-knock.
  Who's there?
Yacht.
  Yacht who?
Yacht's new with you?

Knock-knock.
   Who's there?
Yalta.
   Yalta who?
Yalta know better than to ask that.

♠ ⤢ ➡ ⬐ ⬇ ⬔

Knock-knock.
   Who's there?
Yoda.
   Yoda who?
Yoda best!

   Knock-knock.
      Who's there?
Stu.
      Stu who?
Stu marvelous for words.

♠ ⤢ ➡ ⬐ ⬇ ⬔

Knock-knock.
  Who's there?
Yokum.
  Yokum who?
Yokum a long way, baby.

* * * * * *

Knock-knock.
  Who's there?
Yugo.
  Yugo who?
Yugo on without me.

Knock-knock.
  Who's there?
Eva.
  Eva who?
Eva the best friends must part.

* * * * * *

Knock-knock.
  Who's there?
Yuko.
  Yuko who?
Yuko your way, I'll go mine.

Knock-knock.
  Who's there?
Yukon.
  Yukon who?
Yukon have it, I don't want it.

Knock-knock.
  Who's there?
Yule.
  Yule who?
Yule be sorry.

Knock-knock.
  Who's there?
Yuma.
  Yuma who?
Yuma best friend in the whole world.

Knock-knock.
Who's there?
Yuri.
Yuri who?
"Yuri grand old flag, Yuri high-flying flag."

Knock-knock.
  Who's there?
Zany.
  Zany who?
Zany body seen my girl?

Knock-knock.
  Who's there?
Zeal.
  Zeal who?
Zeal it with a kiss.

Knock-knock.
  Who's there?
Zeke.
  Zeke who?
Zeke and you shall find.

Knock-knock.
  Who's there?
Zinging.
  Zinging who?
"Zinging in the rain."

Knock-knock.
  Who's there?
Zipper.
  Zipper who?
"Zipper de doo dah, zipper de ay."

   ✦   🎵   ➡   🎵   ⬇   ↙

Knock-knock.
  Who's there?
Ziti.
  Ziti who?
Ziti-V is too loud, turn it down.

   ✦   🎵   ➡   🎵   ⬇   ↙

Knock-knock.
  Who's there?
Zoë.
  Zoë who?
Zoë are coming to the end of the book.

   ✦   🎵   ➡   🎵   ⬇   ↙

Knock-knock.
  Who's there?
Zombies.
  Zombies who?
Zombies make honey, zombies don't.

Knock-knock.
Who's there?
Zone.
Zone who?
Zone mother wouldn't know him.

Knock-knock.
 Who's there?
Zookeeper.
 Zookeeper who?
"Zookeeper coming back like a song."

Knock-knock.
 Who's there?
Zoom.
 Zoom who?
"Zoom make me feel so young."

Knock-knock.
 Who's there?
Zounds.
 Zounds who?
Zounds like a good idea to me.

Knock-knock.
  Who's there?
Diesel.
  Diesel who?
Diesel be my last joke.

♠ ♜ ➡ ♜ ⬇ ♜

Knock-knock.
  Who's there?
Zzzya.
  Zzzya who?
Zzzya again my friend. This is the end.

♠ ♜ ➡ ♜ ⬇ ♜

Index